Animal Stories 6

For Families

Observing Animals Around Us

**Collected by
Claire Suminski**

Illustrated by
Susan Swedlund,
and Friends

A special thank you to all our contributing authors, storytellers and guest illustrators!

Donna Nelson
Donna MacDonald
Sue Brown
Kathy Kuhlman
Denise Tiemissen
Gary Shields
Deena Bouknight and
Macon Sense newspaper
Libby Weber

**And to Denise Tiemissen,
our Suminski Family Books proofreader!**

Published by Suminski Family Books

suminskifamilybooks.com

Table of Tales

Don't Feed the Bears! 1
The Great Rescue! 5
Footprints in the Snow 8
Bucket List: A Dude Ranch Adventure 11
Pet the Goose! 15
Sheriff Kathy and Flossie The Wonder Horse:
Part Three in the Flossie Series 19
Miss Sapphire 23
The Elusive Otters of Lake Emory 27
Dog and Bunny "Leap Frog!" 30
Deer Olympics 32
Kool 35
The Firefly Show 44
Making a Firefly Lantern 47
Fireflies: A Poem 48
Observing and Photographing Fireflies 49
Observation Match-Up Game 51
Observing Nature and Keeping a Journal 52
Observing Animals Around Us Word Search ... 54
Answer Sheet 56

Soon we heard very loud howling. It sounded close by! Papaw piped up and said, "Those are wolves!" That made it a little hard to fall asleep!

Don't Feed the Bears!

By Donna Nelson,
as told to Claire Suminski

One summer, when my boys were young, Papaw took us camping at Cades Cove in the Great Smoky Mountains of Tennessee. Before we began our trip, he gave us one very important warning: "Don't feed the bears!" We arrived at our campground at dusk, set up our tent, enjoyed a nice snack, and headed for bed.

As we snuggled into our sleeping bags, it wasn't long before we heard very loud howling. It sounded close by! I told the boys not to worry because it was probably just a pack of coyotes hunting. Papaw piped up and said, "Nope, those are wolves!" That made it a little hard to fall asleep!

The next morning, we got up and fixed a hearty breakfast over our campfire. With the leftover bacon, Papaw made a bacon sandwich for later. He wrapped it in paper and stored it in his pants pocket. I packed some necessities, including water and snacks, in a backpack. Then we cleaned up our breakfast mess, put things away, and headed out for a day of adventure!

We decided to make the five-mile round-trip hike through the hemlock and pine forest to Abram Falls. We drove to the trailhead, which was not far from our campground. As we pulled into the parking lot, I noticed a bear-proof trash receptacle right next to the trailhead. Leaning against the trash receptacle was a wooden sculpture of a bear standing on its hind legs. "Hmm, that's interesting," I thought.

1

Our car was parked, and final preparations for the hike were done; we headed for the trail. Papaw, wanting to sustain himself for the long day, took a couple of big bites of that ole, juicy bacon sandwich that was stored in his pocket.

Just then, the wooden statue of the bear came to life and started heading towards us. It wasn't a statue at all! It was a living and real black bear! And this bear had a radar lock on Papaw's sandwich! "Papaw, he's coming for your sandwich! Throw it down!", I shouted. Papaw said, "No way!" We quickly climbed back in the car and locked the doors. There were FIVE cars between us and that bear. I felt a mix of excitement, fear, and wonder; with a hefty coat of "irritation frosting" all over the top. How could Papaw put us in this dangerous situation?!

The bear climbed on top of the hood of the first car, all the while not taking his eyes off Papaw and his sandwich! We were yelling, "Papaw, get rid of the sandwich!" But to no avail.

"Papaw, get rid of the sandwich!"

The bear climbed from the first car, to the second car, then to the hoods of the third, fourth and fifth. As he got closer, he seemed much bigger! He settled on the hood of our car and stared right through the windshield at Papaw. (Now, readers of this story, let me ask you a question, "Is ANY sandwich worth having a bear crash through your windshield?" "No!!!!" But Papaw had worked hard to make that campfire sandwich, and he was not about to let that black bear steal it from him!)

We started honking the horn, and soon the bear got off the hood of our car and headed into the woods.

You might think we would have given up on the hike and headed back to our campground after our black bear and sandwich escapade, but Papaw still wanted to go to the waterfall. He just wanted to finish that bacon sandwich first!

According to park literature, over 1,500 American Black Bears live in the Great Smoky Mountain National Park. That is an average of two bears per square mile. I am not surprised we came across one! Papaw was right:

"Don't feed the bears!"

In case you are wondering, the five-mile round-trip hike to Abram Falls and back was beautiful and uneventful. We didn't see that bear again! Later, that day, we went to the Cades Cove Visitor Center. They told us all about a special program they had started to reintroduce the Red Wolf to the park. They were currently in captivity and being fed by the rangers each night. So, Papaw was right again: it was wolves we heard that first night! Don't try to feed the wolves either!

The Great Rescue!

by Donna MacDonald

The Kentucky countryside is green and fruitful, and it's filled with a variety of wildlife. Tom and I, along with our four energetic children, lived there for many years, and we all gained a great appreciation of God's creation. We observed the habits of many little critters and large animals, especially deer, which would regularly come through our yard. The woods behind our house, as well as the field and pond off yonder, were rich with deer.

As the seasons and years came and went, our family saw an abundance of does and newborn fawns. We would watch the spotted baby deer grow throughout the spring and summer, slowly losing their spots and looking more like their mom.

One spring morning, as we were watching the activity at our bluebird house, we noticed a little pile of dirt beneath it that hadn't been there before. Upon looking more closely, we realized it was a baby fawn! We watched it for a while. Then, not wanting to disturb it, we went about our day. We kept looking now and then to see if it was still there, and it was!

Louisville
7

Hours passed, and the late spring temperature kept rising. We wondered if the mother deer forgot about her baby fawn. By this time, it was late in the afternoon, so we decided to give the little fawn something to drink. Tom walked out with a bowl of cool, refreshing water. When he got about 10 feet away, that little fawn got up so fast, ran across our yard, then across the neighbor's yard, and finally disappeared into the woods behind it! We were happy to see that the little deer was just fine!

A couple days later, two of our boys were playing near the entrance of the woods while I was on the deck. Suddenly, I heard a very loud sound coming from the woods, like high-pitched bleating. And that's just what it was!

Michael, one of our sons, had lifted the big leaf of a mayapple plant and found the baby deer hiding under it! The little fawn was startled and began bleating loudly. A few seconds later Michael and Andrew came running out of the woods into our yard, not because of the bleating, but because they did not want to get run over! The mother deer heard her fawn's bleating and dashed from one end of the woods all the way to the other, where her little fawn was! She came to the rescue!

Footprints in the Snow

By Claire Suminski

Living in the Southern United States, we do not get a lot of snow. But this was not always the case! Alice, a friend of mine, who is almost 95, grew up in these mountains of Western North Carolina. She shared some wonderful memories with me of her time growing up here, and said that one year there were "seven snows on the ground!" Alice went on to explain the meaning of this phrase. Before the snow from one storm could melt, another storm would come and lay down another layer of fresh snow.

Some of her common "fresh snow" activities were running and sliding on the icy pond, snowball fights, and making delicious snow cream. Her favorite activity was tracking animals in the snow and finding their dens by following their footprints. It was much easier to do this in the snowy winter months than in the warmer months of spring and summer.

Even though I am three decades younger than Alice, I had some of the same experiences growing up. My childhood was spent on the edge of the mountainous Adirondack Park in upstate New York, where the snow on the ground would last well into March! My family and I would go on sledding expeditions in these beautiful New York mountains. Mom would send us off with grilled peanut butter and jelly sandwiches and a Stanley thermos filled with steaming hot chocolate. This kept us fueled for our sledding adventures!

Just like Alice, one of my favorite activities was tracking animals in the snow. One day, while it was snowing and the North wind was blowing, my sister and I followed bunny tracks to an evergreen tree. Its branches were bowing down from the heavy snow. I moved one of the branches to the side and surprised the bunny. It ran off! As we peered between the snow-laden branches, we saw a quiet place they had formed under the tree. This is where the bunny had hidden itself, and stowe decided we could hide here too. We crawled under the branches and sat straight up. It was very quiet there. Any noises were absorbed by the snow.

Soon our Mom came looking for us. She had followed our footprints to our secret hideaway and delivered hot chocolate. We relished every sip and enjoyed just being in this special, silent place.

On another day, while we were trudging up a hill with our sleds through several inches of snow, I noticed that a small animal was moving quickly and quietly under the surface of the snow. I dropped my sled rope and started to follow this nimble creature. It stopped long enough for me to reach down into the snow and gently cup it with my thick, wool-mittened hands. As I pulled my hands back up to the surface, I was surprised to see a little field mouse looking up at me. It looked very scared and tried to escape. I held on and had a good look at the mouse before it squirmed away and tunneled back into the snow. My heart felt lighter having had such a close look at this little animal.

Other animal footprints we would see were from waterfowl and muskrats on the snow-covered frozen pond across from my grandmother's house. And on Grammy's back porch, where she kept her bird feeders, there were many different songbird tracks in the snow. It was easy to see how busy those songbirds had been eating all the fallen sunflower seeds. Alongside their footprints were the large paw prints of her big, fat cats. They often tried to catch the birds, but they were always too slow! Exploring God's handiwork in the beautiful outdoors was exciting. There is so much to be learned from observing animal footprints in the snow!

MY BUCKET LIST: DUDE RANCH ADVENTURE!

By Sue Brown
as told to Claire Suminski

My name is Sue Brown, and I'm 86 years young! My kids asked me what I had on my bucket list. I said that one thing was to go to a dude ranch. So, they took me to The Tennessee Dude and Guest Ranch, just outside of Knoxville.

Probably some of you don't know what a dude ranch is. But if you like riding horses and learning how to take care of them, roasting marshmallows and singing around the campfire, I think you would love it! Plus, being active and outdoors all day makes you sleep very well at night.

Dude ranches first became popular in the late 1800's, and they are still popular today. I think that going to a dude ranch would be a really fun vacation for grandparents to take with their grandchildren.

From start to finish, I will share with you what it was like to be at The Tennessee Dude and Guest Ranch. We were greeted at the gate by two cowgirls on their horses. They were very friendly and helpful. They showed us to our cabin, and we were each assigned to a horse for the whole week. They gave me a gentle beauty, who was white with black spots, named Freckles.

This beautiful painting is by Sue Brown.

We woke up early every morning. At 6:00 AM I mucked out my horse's stall and fed her. My tools of the trade were a pitchfork and wheelbarrow. Then we ate breakfast. Notice that we had to feed our horse first. That was a good lesson.

Cookie, the camp cook, would pack a lunch for each one of us every day: a sandwich and a cookie for us and a carrot for our horse.

The first day, we practiced riding around in a ring. (There was a set of stairs to help us get up on our horses.) After that, it was a different trail every day.

Out on the trail, we saw deer, squirrels and rabbits. One day, a horse ahead of me in line got spooked, and the horses all had a chain reaction. That was a little scary. A special part of our time on the trail was at break time when the owner and his wife would have a short Bible study.

At the end of our ride, I would take care of Freckle's saddle, brush her down, clean her hooves, and feed and water her. Sometimes I would hose her down and dry her off. Then it was time for me to rest!

At suppertime, we would eat chow prepared by Cookie at a covered chuck wagon. I think that everything tastes better outside, especially around a campfire. We would have things like barbeque, chili, hot dogs, and camp stew-all cooked over the fire. We would sing campfire songs while roasting marshmallows.

There were wonderful college kids working there for the season. They helped us with our horses, taught Bible study lessons, and some of them played guitars around the campfire.

The last night, we said goodbye to our horses, went home to our cabins and packed up. We left early the next morning to go home. Being outdoors, making new friends, having quiet time to think and pray and riding my sweet horse every day-it all added up to one of the best vacations I have ever had. And that is saying a lot for a woman who is 86 years young!

I hope you all get to go to a dude ranch some time. Maybe I'll see you there, because I want to go back! In the meantime, "Happy Trails to You!"

by Claire Suminski

Have you ever enjoyed doing something so much that you thought everyone else must love it too? Well, that's how my husband felt about fishing in Kansas.

On our very first wedding anniversary, in mid-July, Joe took me on a fishing trip in the dusty sand dunes of Kansas. We camped by a small lake. Up until then, my experience with camping had been in the Adirondacks of upstate New York. The large, beautiful lakes were deep, cool, and refreshing, shaded by an abundance of trees and gently sloping mountains.

This Kansas lake we camped near was so small that it was more like a large pond. And to my surprise when we arrived, there was no shade because there were no trees! We got our camp all set up and made our supper over a campfire and then settled down for the night. The next morning, we woke to pleasant temperatures, but being familiar with Kansas summer weather, I knew the temperature would quickly rise. We packed our gear in the canoe, including two fishing poles and set out on the pond. As we glided along, I ran my fingers just below the surface of the water and discovered that it was lukewarm.

So far, our day had consisted of Joe fishing and me watching him fish. For a while, I sat quietly in the canoe, feeling very proud of my husband for being such a fine outdoorsman. I admired his deeply tanned skin, the result of many hours spent outside. My own skin, however, was very pale because I spent so much time working inside. By 10:00 a.m., I noticed that my skin was being burned by the hot Kansas sun, and my feelings of admiration were fading into feelings of boredom as I sat in the canoe on this small, unshaded, lukewarm lake. I noticed that there were a couple dozen Canada Geese swimming nearby. Suddenly, an idea occurred to me. I looked at Joe and said, "I bet you can't catch one of those geese!" I knew that my husband loved a challenge. So, before I could say "Pigs in a blanket," he was out of the canoe and swimming after those geese!

Now, my situation was worse! I was not only hot and bored— I was all alone in the canoe. I regretted laying down that dare, but Joe was happily taking on the adventure! He reached the shore with the frantic geese less than a yard ahead of him. Then, the geese hurried over the top of a sand dune straight ahead, with Joe in hot pursuit.

Only a couple of minutes passed before I saw Joe's head emerge at the top of the dune with a triumphant look in his eyes. As he crested the dune, I could see he was carrying a bewildered goose upside down by its feet, its wings flapping wildly.

"Was that a smirk on his face?", I wondered. He shifted the goose under his arm, carrying it like a football, and started to wade through the water to meet me. Looking at him, he reminded me of a victorious warrior having come from battle! As he got closer, I could not imagine what would happen next.

He stood chest-deep in the water next to the canoe; the goose grasped firmly in both hands. Then he thrust the goose towards me and said, "Claire, pet the goose!"

We have been married for forty years now. Most of our anniversaries have been variations of fine dining in air conditioning. We celebrate the love that brought us together and laugh about the things that make us different. But no anniversary has ever compared to our very first one, when I got to pet a Canada Goose!

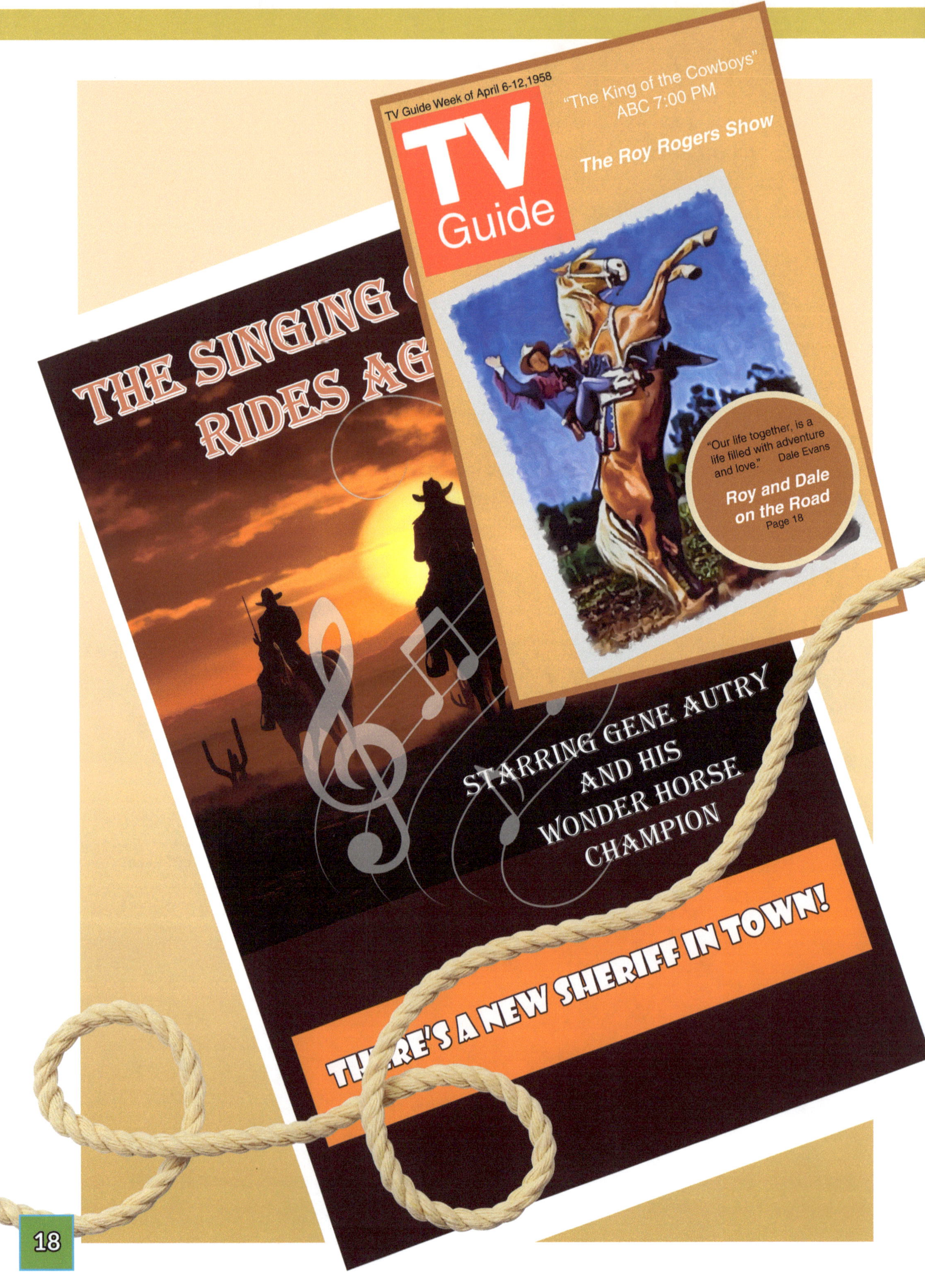
TV Guide Week of April 6-12,1958
"The King of the Cowboys"
ABC 7:00 PM
The Roy Rogers Show
TV Guide
"Our life together, is a life filled with adventure and love."   Dale Evans
Roy and Dale on the Road
Page 18
THE SINGING COWBOY RIDES AGAIN
STARRING GENE AUTRY AND HIS WONDER HORSE CHAMPION
THERE'S A NEW SHERIFF IN TOWN!

SHERIFF KATHY AND FLOSSIE THE WONDER HORSE

Part Three in the Flossie Series
An Interview with Kathy Kuhlman

Written by Claire Suminski

Kathy Kuhlman was the Macon County 4-H agent for several years while the Suminski children were growing up. She was so good at working with young people and bringing out the best in each one of them. Her North Dakota farm-girl sense of humor always shone through. A lot of her fine qualities come from being raised in a tight-knit, hardworking family in which she was able to engage her vivid imagination as she played outdoors. This usually involved her family's black and white Shetland Pony named Flossie!

At the time Kathy was growing up, Roy Rogers and his palomino Thoroughbred mix named Trigger were possibly Hollywood's most famous cowboy and horse team. They did the stunts in their movies, and Roy said that Trigger was so sure footed, he never slipped or fell. Not only was Trigger very sure footed, he was intelligent and gentle with people.

Kathy and I had a wonderful time reminiscing about her times playing "Sheriff Kathy" with Flossie as her loyal steed.

Claire: Kathy, how would you and Flossie try and imitate Roy Rogers and Trigger?

Kathy: Well, I would jump "Flossie the Wonder Horse" over logs and ride through streams in pursuit of "the bad guys" as we played out our own story lines. Every day was a new adventure!

Claire: Let's see, besides Roy Rogers and Trigger, who else did you and Flossie pretend to be?

Kathy: Well, there was Roy's wife, Dale, and her buckskin Quarter Horse, Buttercup. Buttercup was a beauty and could actually outrun Trigger.   The Lone Ranger had a pure white Thoroughbred Quarter Horse, Silver, and Gene Autry rode a Tennessee Walking Horse, Champion. All of these duos starred in TV Westerns that were popular at the time.

Claire: Did you have a favorite?

Kathy: That would be Roy Rogers. He was the "King of the Cowboys." He was one of the good guys who wore a white hat and was always on the right side of the law, fighting the bad guys. Roy would often sing songs as he rode, and so I also would sing as Flossie and I rode along the trail.

Claire: What did your family think of your role play? And more importantly, did Flossie like it?

Kathy: My family was not likely aware of my dramatic productions. But they knew I was out enjoying time with my pony. Little did they know I was "protecting the farm from the bad guys." Flossie seemed to enjoy the ride, until she would get tired, thirsty, or hungry, and then wanted to get back to the pasture to be with her friends. That's when I would see another side of Flossie!

Claire: Outdoor adventures were a very important part of my youth. Do you have any thoughts for young families today about children benefitting from outdoor play?

Kathy: It is a concern of mine that children are being deprived of the benefits of enjoying the great outdoors. Outdoor activity opens up opportunities to build life skills: it increases physical health, builds emotional well-being, increases appreciation and respect for nature, and encourages imagination and creativity. A horseback ride or a walk in the woods far surpasses staring at a screen for recreation.

Claire: You have made some great points, Kathy. I think that many of our readers really see the benefit to spending time outdoors!
I have a question about Flossie. Famous TV horse personalities were known for being calm and easy for their riders and fans to get along with.   How about Flossie?

Kathy: Well, Flossie was a great horse to ride, but she was also known to have a dark side. She could be the sneakiest, meanest, most intelligent, and conniving Shetland Pony of ALL times. When she was tired of hauling me and my friends or cousins around, she would go through her bag of tricks to get us "off her back." Her methods included a run through the trees, a duck under my brother's chinning bar, a sideswipe of the fence, a fast squeeze through a slightly open barn door, or dumping us into the water trough. She would achieve this by running quickly to the water trough and immediately stopping, and putting her head down, which would jettison the rider into the water! She would never give any warning as to when this might happen, so I had to be on my toes to recognize it and protect myself from the "Flossie Treatment."

Claire: Well, that may be why she did not make it to Hollywood! But I know you loved her very much.

Kathy: Yes, Flossie had many tricks "up her sleeve," but I loved her anyway.   As a result of my riding experiences with Flossie, I "graduated" to larger horses and competed in 4-H shows, horse shows, and fairs. Flossie was a great part of my childhood.

Miss Sapphire

Written by Donna MacDonald

Early spring had arrived in Kentucky, and it was time to plan our garden. Questions like "What vegetables and fruits are our favorites?" and "Should we grow something different this year?" often came up while my family and I planned the garden. This particular year, my 12-year-old daughter, Abigail, exclaimed, "Let's grow some butterflies!" I wasn't sure what she meant, but she explained that she had read in one of her nature books that certain butterflies are attracted to specific plants. We researched which butterflies lived in our area and what plants they liked to eat.

There were many pretty options, but we especially liked the black swallowtail butterfly. It had such lovely blue spots on its black wings. So, that's the butterfly we decided to raise. Parsley was one of its favorite foods; growing swallowtail butterflies and parsley sounded simple enough - and so our adventure began!

As the weeks went by, our garden flourished. We kept a special eye on our little parsley plants. They were growing as fast as weeds! Occasionally, we noticed the black swallowtail butterfly on the parsley. Then we noticed a few tiny brown eggs on the plants. We watered the parsley diligently and watched carefully for pesky insects. We certainly did not want those in our garden!

There was one insect that we *did* want in our garden, though, and one day we finally saw it! It was a small black-and-yellow-striped caterpillar that had hatched from one of the tiny brown eggs and was feeding on our parsley plants! The next day we saw two more. They were the little fellows that we were all waiting for! We watched them grow as they continued to munch on their favorite food.

When the caterpillars were big enough, it was time to take one of them and put it in a jar so we could watch the wonderful change that would take place in this little insect's life! We put a few drops of water in the bottom of the jar, put plenty of parsley on top, and poked holes in the lid to let some air in. Our black-and-yellow-striped friend seemed happy, and it had plenty to eat!

After a few days, we noticed that our caterpillar friend, "Stripey," attached itself to the lid of the jar. Soon after that, it began to take a very long nap. While sleeping, the caterpillar went through an amazing change! Eventually, its striped skin began to crack open, and a greenish-brown body, which was slightly shiny and hard like a beetle's body, came out.

There hung Stripey in a jar on an end table in our den. We all hoped it was still alive, but it was hard to tell, since it didn't move at all. We forgot about it at times. But one day, as we were sitting around in the den, Abigail observed something black coming out of the end of the hard shell. Stripey was alive and began to emerge from its chrysalis! We watched it wiggle, crack open the chrysalis, and squeeze all the way out! Stripey had become a black swallowtail butterfly—and a very beautiful one at that! After it hung upside down at the top of the jar for a few minutes, we realized that we needed to put it outside. We set the jar right in the middle of the parsley plants and took off the lid. A little while later, it flew to some of the nearby plants.

While we were watching the beautiful black swallowtail butterfly, we became certain that "Stripey" needed a name change. It was no longer a striped caterpillar; it had become a lovely butterfly. "Miss Sapphire" seemed to be the perfect name for her. Every time she flew to our garden that summer, we'd call out, "Miss Sapphire!"

Metamorphosis

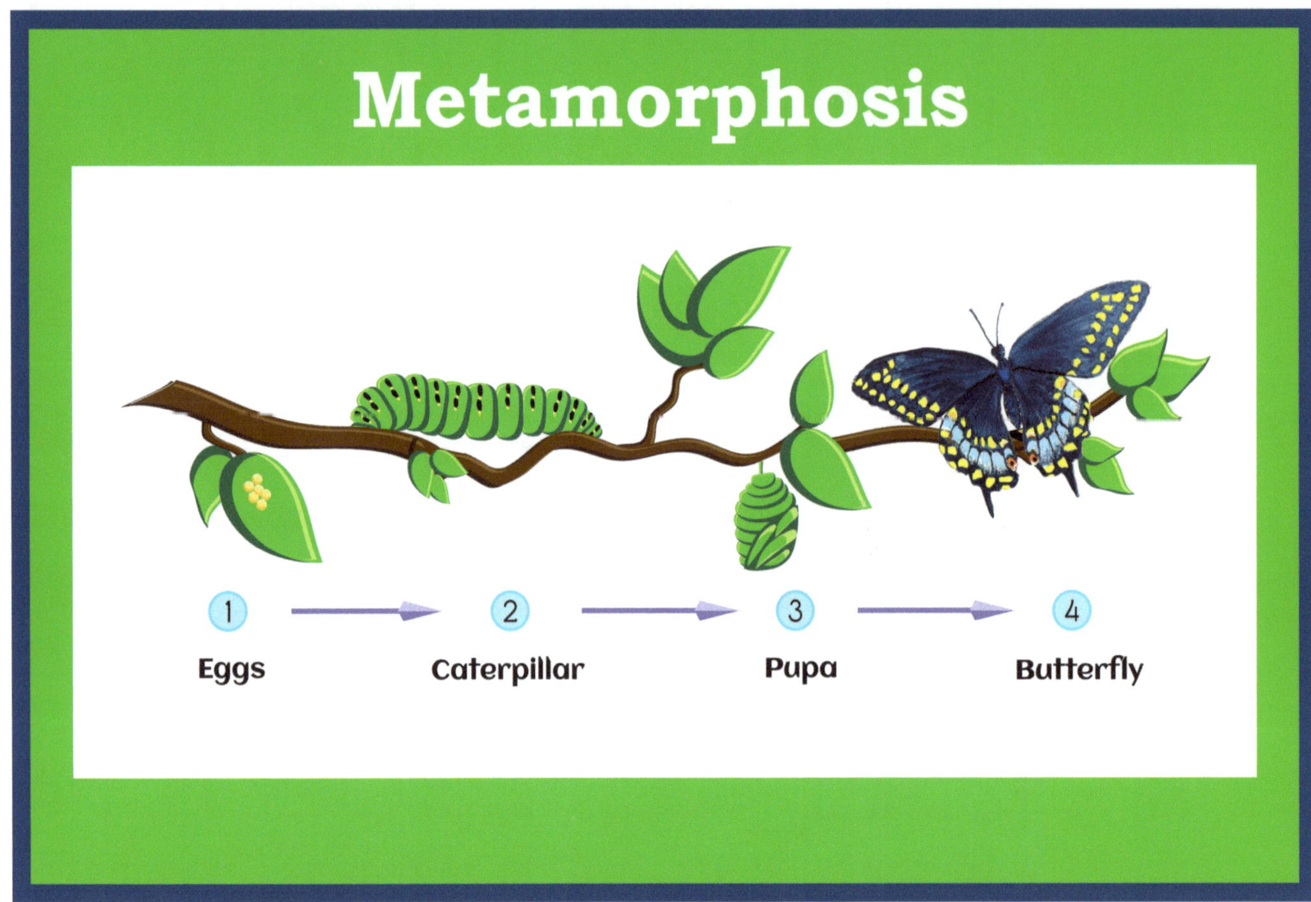

***The transformation of a caterpillar into a butterfly is called metamorphosis. This word comes from the Greek word *metamorphe*. The related verb, *metamorphoō*, is found in Romans 12:2 where it is translated as "transformed."

Romans 12:2 (NKJV) And do not be conformed to this world, but be transformed by the renewing of your mind, that you may prove what *is* that good and acceptable and perfect will of God.

In Romans 12:2, to be transformed refers to the change that takes place in the life of a child of God as they put on God's Word in their mind and heart and believe it.

The Elusive Otters of Lake Emory

by Claire Suminski

After several years of sharing stories about the American Bald Eagles nesting on Lake Emory, my family and neighbors started branching out and sharing more accounts of other wildlife that have made this reservoir their home.

I have always been fascinated by otters but seldom saw them in the wild. One day as I was walking along the shoreline, I observed two animals swimming quickly down the center of the lake. Their movements were very fluid and serpent-like as they looped in and out of the water, steadily moving towards Lake Emory Dam.

I was transfixed and could not take my eyes off them, as I hurried down the road, trying to keep up with them. Were they otters? What else could they be? I decided that they must be very powerful swimmers because as they reached the edge of the dam, they were not sucked in by the current. They disappeared under water, resurfacing at the rocks along the far shore. They then scrambled across the rocks and around the dam. I rushed to the area just below the dam, where the Little Tennessee River runs freely, hoping that I would still be able to see this pair of sleek, furry animals. They did not stop to rest but kept moving steadily until they reached a sandy spot along the river's edge and then disappeared into the vegetation. I was thrilled! They were clearly otters!

I kept watch and at times after that, I would see them fishing in the lake. One day I saw an otter carry a fish up on a log and then tear chunks off to eat. Another day, I saw one floating on its back, holding fresh prey on its stomach while hungrily eating it. I was standing only about 20 yards away and was sure the otter could see me, but it did not seem afraid. It later disappeared under the roots of a large tree along the shore. In fact, a young outdoorsman I know was fishing on the takeout dock by the Lake Emory Dam at dusk, and an otter came up out of the water and knocked over his bait bucket and ate the contents. The young man was so surprised, he almost fell off the dock into over 15 feet of water! Other fishermen report seeing the otters active at dusk and dawn, which is encouraging.

My neighbor, Linda, observed the eagles dive-bombing the otters. Both were after fish, but the eagles wanted to chase off their competition! For a few months, it seemed that the otters had relocated. This is not surprising as river otters can cover a large territory and have multiple dens.

For a period of time, one of my daughters regularly kayaked Lake Emory in the early evening after work. She shared that one of the otters would follow alongside her boat as she paddled, sometimes bumping the hull of her kayak. She knew better than to reach out and touch a wild animal but enjoyed this view of an otter's social side.

Nature always has to be ready to adapt in order to survive. The best way to see wildlife is to go outside and make quiet observations of your surroundings, especially at dusk and dawn. I am still watching for the otters and am sure they will be back.

Dog and Bunny
"Leap Frog!"

By Denise Tiemissen

Zoē was a Rat Terrier that my family had for a long time. She lived to be 17 years old! We got her when she was just a puppy. Rat Terriers were originally bred to hunt and catch vermin like rats and foxes and rabbits. The word "terrier" comes from an old French word meaning "ground" or "earth." These dogs are so tenacious when hunting that they are willing to burrow into the ground to go after unwanted pests. They are also very energetic dogs. Zoē was so bouncy that it seemed as if her legs were spring-loaded!

Although Zoē was a Rat Terrier, she never went after outdoor pests. Instead, she was the most playful, friendly dog you could ever meet. She played with people—she loved playing fetch with anyone—and she played with all animals, even pesky varmints. Nobody was a stranger to Zoē!

One day, Zoē was visiting our neighbor across the street. The neighbor had a very big Blue Spruce pine tree in their front yard, with sweeping branches that stretched all the way to the ground. Zoē was playfully running around the tree, when we noticed that a bunny rabbit was also circling the tree. Soon, Zoē and the bunny started playing a game of leapfrog—jumping over each other, all around the tree, over and over again. They never seemed to tire of this fun activity. We were all amazed at what we were seeing: a dog who was supposed to chase and catch vermin was playing with one and having fun!

Deer Olympics!

By Claire Suminski

My friend, Glenda, and I both love to watch deer, and we swap stories about them. I watch the Lake Emory deer, and she observes the Wayah Road deer.

One day she asked me if I ever noticed the deer playing games with each other. Then she described in wonderful detail a time when she saw them. The deer formed two lines facing each other, then ran toward the middle, reared up on their hind legs, and waved their hooves. This description piqued my interest, and I really wanted to see it for myself someday.

During one of my deer watching adventures in the Watauga community, I saw deer playing a chasing game. It looked as if they were taking turns chasing each other, jumping, and then turning in the air! It was fun to watch!

Another story that Glenda shared with me involved her neighbor and his large dog. While on her porch one morning, she saw a remarkable example of "Deer Olympics" unfold before her.

She saw her neighbor and his leashed dog running together. Her neighbor wore tan sweat pants, a tan sweatshirt, and a tan hat, and his big dog was tan, too.

As Glenda watched, she noticed a deer coming down from the side of the hill, running after them as if they were part of the herd. When the deer caught up with the running duo, all three were startled! They stopped, looked at each other, then the deer ran off as fast as she could!

Deer are usually afraid of canines. And most canines love to chase deer! It's a good thing the dog was on a leash!

Stories like these make me want to observe wildlife even more. You never know what you are going to see!

Painting of Gary Shields and Kool
by Sheila Moffitt

By Claire Suminski   From an interview with Gary Shields

Gary Shields, a young, very brave Army paratrooper from the mountains of Western North Carolina befriended an equally brave Australian Basenji, named Kool. They served together during the Vietnam War and survived side by side in that war-torn country. Kool alerted Gary and his team to danger many times over.

As a high school student, Gary watched paratroopers from Fort Bragg's 82nd Airborne Division conducting parachute training jumps in the mountainous terrain. He knew that someday "that would be him." Although he had never flown in a plane, he had set his mind to become a paratrooper. Gary received his draft notice after high school graduation and enlisted in the Army. He eventually served with the 173rd Airborne Brigade in the Vietnam War. That is where he met Kool.

Gary was the son of a Baptist minister. He grew up believing that devotion to faith, family and country was essential. Raised on a farm with a variety of working dogs—hound dogs, beagles, and fox dogs—he learned that every family member and farm animal contributed to the family's livelihood and success. He also learned how to work with his hands, use good common sense, and treat others with respect.

Through his many years of post-war service in our town, I have known Gary to be a man of vision, strength, and compassion—deeply rooted in faith and understanding the power of teamwork. I asked him how he came to know and work with this wonderful dog named Kool, and how he grew as a leader while serving in the Army.

In the 173rd Airborne Brigade, Gary was part of a squad doing reconnaissance in the Vietnam jungle. The enemy was ever-present. They had to be on their toes all the time and not give away their position. One day, as his team was crossing an irrigation ditch filled with chest-high, moving water, he saw an animal swimming towards him. At first, he thought it might be a mongoose, but as it got closer, he realized it was a young dog. The canine took to him right away, so Gary put the pup up on his shoulders, around his neck and continued crossing. It was very hot and muggy, and the pup felt cool on his neck. He decided to call him, "Kool," and the name stuck.

Gary soon realized that Kool was an Australian Basenji—a breed of hunting dog that could not bark due to the shape of its larynx. A sharp breed of dog—one who could recognize danger but would not bark—was exactly what was needed. The Australians were allies of the United States, with troops stationed in the jungle as well. They had recently changed positions and must have left this young dog behind. It was the Australians' loss and the Americans' gain! As time passed, they found this quiet dog to be a very important part of their team. Basenjis are known for their courage, intelligence and speed. These qualities held true with Kool, and he grew to be indispensable to their team!

During patrols, Kool would stay close to Gary. The hair on his neck would bristle if he heard or caught the scent of the enemy approaching. As a hunting dog breed, Kool's eyes, nose and ears were sharper than those of the soldiers. Kool became a tremendous boost to their field detection skills and awareness! When going through a swamp, Gary would place Kool on his shoulders around his neck and position himself in the center of the team. Each soldier had a loop of string around his pinkie finger, and the string was connected to Gary. If Gary felt Kool's hair bristle, he would pull on the string in both directions, and his full team would be alerted. He is sure that this saved their lives more than once.

When they stopped to eat, Gary and the other soldiers shared their rations with Kool, as no real dog food was available. Kool ate whatever he was given without complaint. At night, when it was time to go to sleep, each man would dig a trench to lie in and pile the dirt up like a berm along one side. Kool slept, pressed up against Gary's side. Basenjis tend to be "one-man dogs" and stick by their masters.

One night, Kool woke Gary up. They were both on high alert. Gary sensed that a wild animal was close by. Dirt had fallen on top of him from the berm. What was it? The next morning, when he and Kool got up, they found a giant python right next to their makeshift camp—nothing to fool around with. If Kool had not been there, the python might have wrapped himself around Gary, suffocating him in his sleep!

Many dangers lurked in the jungle. How grateful they were for Kool's attentive, hunting dog ways. Time after time, he proved himself to be an important part of their team.

As the time grew closer for Gary's departure from Viet Nam, he knew that he would have to say goodbye to Kool. He could not take him out of the country. Gary's red-haired brother-in-arms from West Virginia would take over Kool's care. Kool would stay where he belonged, continuing his job as a working dog and helping to keep the soldiers in Gary's platoon safe.

Gary said that many prayers were offered by his family and friends when he left to fight for our freedom in the Vietnam War. He was injured three times, and recovered each time and received three Purple Heart medals. Gary Shields returned home safely and was ready to live a life of service in this community for decades to come. He remains forever thankful for those answered prayers and for the little dog the Australians left behind, named Kool.

GARY SHIELDS recently shared photographs in the telling of his story about a dog that became an unlikely companion and protector while he served in the Vietnam War. Even pulling out photographs of his time in Vietnam was a tenuous exercise, he admitted.

However, sharing positive stories is a balm for veterans, and Shields hopes children and young people will be inspired and encouraged.

"I'm very involved with veterans on a regular basis," he said. "We also have to be supportive of today's soldiers and students and encourage them whether they are in the workforce or the military." He added that stories like this will hopefully teach younger generations about history and also provide a glimpse of what life was like for soldiers in Vietnam.

MACON SENSE

May 8, 2025   *Your Community, Your Stories*   Vol. 2, Issue 16

Soldier finds a 'God-send' in a Vietnam Jungle

By Deena Bouknight
May 8, 2025
Re-printed by permission

When 21-year-old Gary Shields saw something move as he and other soldiers in Vietnam were crossing a stream, he immediately became alert. The dangers in the Asian jungle were real and ever-present. What emerged was a dog – an uncommon sight in the war-torn country. The dog swam to him, he put it on his shoulder, and they crossed to the other side together. "It was so hot and that wet dog was so cool on my neck and shoulders," said Shields. "So, I named him Kool."

That was 57 years ago. Since that time in Vietnam, Shields has served 37 years in education, with 29 spent with the Macon County School System – 21 of which were as principal at Franklin High School.

He also spent those decades in numerous capacities as a public servant for the town and Macon County, including 11 years as a Macon County Commissioner and four years on the Board of Education. Yet, despite his full plate of career and volunteer accomplishments, Shields still remembers the dog clearly and fondly. "It turned out to be a God-send because it was an Australian Basenji and they can't bark," he said. In fact, because of the shape of their larynxes, these dogs are considered "barkless." Shields and the other soldiers deduced that the dog must have been left behind by Australian soldiers who had previously been in the area. Kool ended up staying with Shields and regularly alerting him and the other soldiers during OPs (Observation Patrols during the day) and LPs (Listening Patrols at night) simply by bristling the hair on its neck when danger was afoot.   (Continued on next page)

GARY SHIELDS in Vietnam with Kool, an Australian Basenji, that ended up his companion for a time while deployed.

SOLDIERS IN the Vietnam War often had to cross streams like the one where Gary Shields first discovered the dog he would name Kool.

Claire Suminski, a local author and publisher of Suminski Family Books, got wind of Shields's unique Vietnam dog companion story and decided to include it in the upcoming "Animal Stories" series, sixth edition. "We hope to have Gary's story featured on the cover," said Suminski.

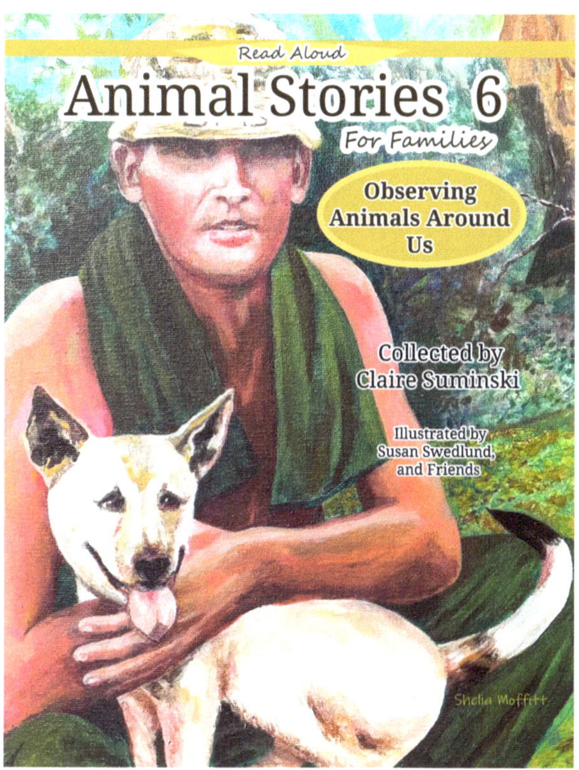

Kool was a bright spot in a dark place. "When you have buddies killed, you stop connecting," Shields shared. "Kool made things more bearable. He was a special piece of my experience there [in Vietnam]." Shields enlisted in the Army in the fall of 1966, after graduating high school and receiving his draft notice. "I knew I needed to be in for three years to get the GI bill to pay for four years of college – the only way I was going to college."

He had been enamored with the Airborne division of the Army ever since the 82nd Airborne out of Fort Bragg used the dairy farm field (now the site of the Macon County Airport) as a drop zone for paratroopers, which Shields observed when he was in the 9th grade." I had never ridden in a plane, but I wanted to be in the Airborne," said Shields.

He finished basic training at Fort Bragg, N.C., communications school at Fort Gordon, Ga., and then attended jump school at Fort Benning, Ga. From there he cross-trained with the 10th Special Forces in Germany to become a well-rounded soldier. His training equipped him as a radio operator, for combat weaponry, as well as for handling mortars and conducting reconnaissance. Then he was assigned combat duty with the 173rd Airborne Brigade in the Vietnam War. He served 18 months total, with a month break back in the United States. Kool was with him 15 out of those 18 months. "He was with me everywhere I went, and he protected our group several times. He provided comfort. Animals have that effect on us." Shields was wounded three times and was awarded three Purple Hearts as well as other distinctions. When Shields visited home and when he was recovering from injuries, Kool stayed with a fellow soldier friend he called "Red." "I accepted the fact that Kool would not be able to go home [to the United States] with me," said Shields. "Animals could not be taken out of the country." He said his final good-bye to Kool in May 1969.

He was in college in September of that same year when he received word that Kool had been killed in a cross-fire exchange at a camp. Apparently, the enemy had tripped the containment wire around the camp and the noise had caused Kool to run out into the open to investigate. "It was sad to hear, but I tried to put it out of my mind, which you have to do when you've served in a war," said Shields.

From painting to book

Before becoming featured in the upcoming "Animal Stories 6" book, Shields and Kool were first the subject of a painting by Shelia Moffitt created a few years ago. Annually, Macon County Art Association has hosted a Veterans Portrait Project Program that honors selected war veterans with a portrait, painted by a local artist, based on a photograph. Moffitt (now deceased) used a black and white photograph of Shields with Kool to achieve a color painting of the two. The painting hangs in Shields's home.

Anna and Gary Shields and daughter, Lindsay

Suminski learned about the portrait and the story surrounding it. "I asked if I could interview Gary Shields for one of our 'Animal Stories' book, and he enthusiastically said 'Yes.'"   She added, "I think that Gary's time serving during Vietnam really shaped him as a leader. And throughout my 34 years of living in Franklin, he has been a champion in the protection and guidance of children, young adults, and families. This is just a great story."

"Animal Stories 6" should be out in Spring of 2026, according to Suminski. When this book is published, a portion of the proceeds of the initial sales is donated to a local nonprofit. This time funds will be donated to Kid's Place.

This has grown to be a very important arm of giving for our family in this community," said Suminski. All of the published "Animal Stories" books and other Suminski Family Books, including the Cowee Sam series, can be found at www.suminskifamilybooks.com.

The Firefly Show

Lampyridae Family Fun

by Claire Suminski

When my husband and I were raising our family,watching fireflies after sunset was one of our favorite early summer pastimes. The kids would gently catch several little lightning bugs to put in mason jars with hole-punched lids. The jars then became firefly-fueled lanterns. Before bedtime, we would let them go.

Fireflies are beetles that belong to the Lampyridae family, with over 2000 individual species! Our Grandpa Carl once saw hundreds of fireflies in a tall oak tree beside the river, sparkling like tiny holiday lights. This spectacle can happen during mating season because fireflies attract mates with their bioluminescent lights flashing off and on. Some species flash in a synchronized fashion.

One year we organized a group of about 15 friends and went to see the synchronized firefly display in Elkmont, Tennessee. First we signed up online for a shuttle that would take us from the Sugarlands Visitor Center to Elkmont, which costs $1. In the years to come, word got out about these special fireflies and so many people wanted to go see them that they had to establish a lottery system! We reached our destination by 6:00 pm and had a few hours to enjoy a deep, roaring mountain stream complete with huge boulders to climb on.   Right after we climbed back up to the pathway, a big, beautiful black bear crossed the stream right where we had been playing. What an experience!

Elkmont Tennessee Firefly Show – Right after we had been playing in the stream!!!

By 9:30 PM, fireflies were ready to put on their show. The emailed instructions said that only flashlights with red cellophane over them, to defuse the light, would be allowed. We did not want to deter the fireflies from putting on their show and were prepared with our red lights. At first the flashing seemed random, but as the minutes passed, these little beetles would flash 6-8 times and then go dark for about 8 seconds. All at the same time! It was thrilling!

After an hour, the fireflies were still going strong, but the rangers started herding us back to the shuttles. I could have stayed until the wee hours of the night. However, the rangers didn't want anyone to get lost in the dark, and they were ready to go home!

How to Make a Fire Fly Lantern

Equipment:
  *Quart mason jar with holes punched in lid or a "Sprout Lid"

What to do:

Right at dusk on an early summer evening, head out to the yard to look for fireflies.

Put a little grass in the bottom of a quart jar. Walk around the yard and when you see a firefly, catch it with your hand. Transfer it into your quart jar and put the lid on. It usually doesn't take long to collect several in your jar. It is so fun to hold it up and watch the fireflies blink. Also, as the evening grows darker, your jar really will be like a lantern!

Remember to handle them gently and let them go at the end of the night.

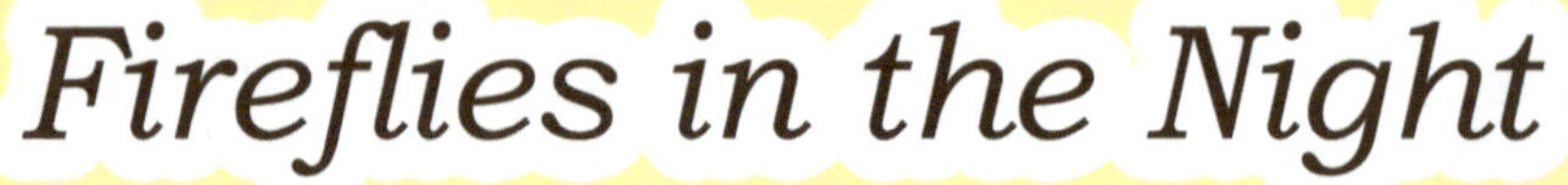

Fireflies in the Night

by Libby Weber

I have patiently waited for your arrival
Camera in hand as I set out to explore
To find the most hidden of places
Where your illuminating forms will appear

In anticipation of your arrival
As the darkness replaces the light
I'm here anxiously waiting
In the silence of the night

But wait! What's that I see
One tiny light all on its own
Be patient I tell myself
This firefly can't be alone

Without introduction,
And in the blink of my eye
The mating ritual is beginning
Fireflies are glowing in the night

I am captivated by the splendor
Surrounding me this night
As my camera freezes the movement
Of the mystical display of lights

Then suddenly without warning
I am alone here where I stand
No sight of the tiny fireflies
This wonderful time has come to an end

So, until our next encounter
I will leave this magical scene
Good-bye to all the fireflies
I will see you in my dreams....

Observing and Photographing Fireflies

by Libby Weber

I began my love for fireflies a few years ago when a friend of mine invited me to go to Elkmont to observe and photograph their mating ritual.   What I saw was a spectacular show of fireflies illuminating and searching for their perfect mates; one that I will never forget. I didn't get any firefly shots that night but I have a priceless memory of something quite amazing.

After coming home, I did a bit of reading as to what other photographers do to prepare for photographing fireflies, and what equipment they use. I researched and experimented and came up with a process that works for me.

I like to scout out where the best location is to photograph fireflies. Because fireflies typically hang out in wooded areas and near water, I search for that same type of setting (and get as close as possible). Most importantly, I arrive BEFORE dark. The equipment that I use is my tripod, camera, lens, wireless shutter release and a red-light flash light (backup batteries are good to have as well). I also take red cellophane to put over the lights and screen on my camera because bright lights can disrupt the mating of the fireflies. I make sure my camera battery is fully charged and both of my camera cards are cleared.   I also take rain gear to protect my equipment (and myself) should it rain during my shoot.

.

Fireflies usually start lighting up around 9:30 (in Franklin, NC), so I set up my tripod and camera around 8:30, then I take a few shots (on auto focus) right before sunset for my base photo (the base shot is one that will show some definition of the surroundings). Once I feel satisfied with the base shot, I set my camera to manual mode. Because the lighting changes as it gets darker. I continue to adjust my ISO until it's really dark outside. (Bulb, F2.8, ISO around 1250 but can change depending on ambient light).   A lot of photographers will set their camera to automatically take interval shots of fireflies, but I like to use my cable release to control the time for each shot. It's a lot more work, but I have more success doing it this way.   Once I start photographing the fireflies, I continue on until I feel I have enough photos to photo stack them (around an hour).   Photo stacking is a process by which multiple photos are aligned and stacked using a photo editing software; I use Adobe Light Room Classic and Adobe Photoshop.

For me, I keep it simple; it's a journey of learning. Most importantly, I enjoy witnessing these beautiful creatures in all their splendor as they put on a light show like no other.

Here is one of my favorite firefly photos..

Observation Match-up Game

Think back at what kinds of things you observed and learned from each story. Match the story with the appropriate letter and write it on the line provided (the first one has been done for you.) You can write your answers on a piece of scrap paper if you don't want to write them in your book.

Story		Match
Pet the Goose	I	**A** Baby deer and Momma
Fireflies		**B** How to brush a horse
Dog and Bunny "Leapfrog!"		**C** Deer playing games
My Bucket List: Dude Ranch Adventures		**D** Excellent swimmers
Kool		**E** Why some bugs light up
Don't Feed the Bears!		**F** Following tracks
The Great Rescue		**G** What happens when bears smell food
Deer Olympics		**H** Metamorphosis
Sheriff Kathy and Flossie the Wonder Horse		**I** Can fly and swim
The Elusive Otters of Lake Emory		**J** TV show partners
Miss Sapphire		**K** Dog keeping soldiers safe
Footprints in the Snow		**L** Jumping partners

Observing Nature and Keeping a Journal

Excerpt from Chapter 3 of "Cowee Sam and the Eagles' Nest"

"The eagles are so beautiful flying over the river and I want to learn more about them. If you show me what to do, I will watch the eagles every day after school. I would love to help you," Annie insisted.

"Great! Scientific observation can be very fun," Molly pointed out. "We're receiving knowledge of the outside world through our senses and then recording what we observe. We'll use some scientific instruments to help us, like a thermometer outside the window so we can record the temperature and weather for that day, and powerful binoculars so we can watch the eagles closely without disturbing their activities. We can write all our observations down in this notebook, and then we'll set up our 'Observation Post' here at the farmhouse."

Jerome offered, "I will help you gather the equipment and get things set up."

"Thanks, Jerome!" Molly replied.

"Okay! I can write down what I see, Aunt Molly." Annie suddenly got a concerned look on her face, "But what if I don't understand what it is that I'm seeing? What if the eagles do something and I don't know what they're doing?"

"Wow Annie, that is a wonderful question! Are you sure you're not a scientist already? Because that is exactly what scientists do; they ask questions. Sometimes answers are found through observation, but there are also research books to consult."

Annie looked relieved and smiled as she said, "I'm very excited to learn all about our new neighbors, the eagles. And to welcome the babies when they hatch!"

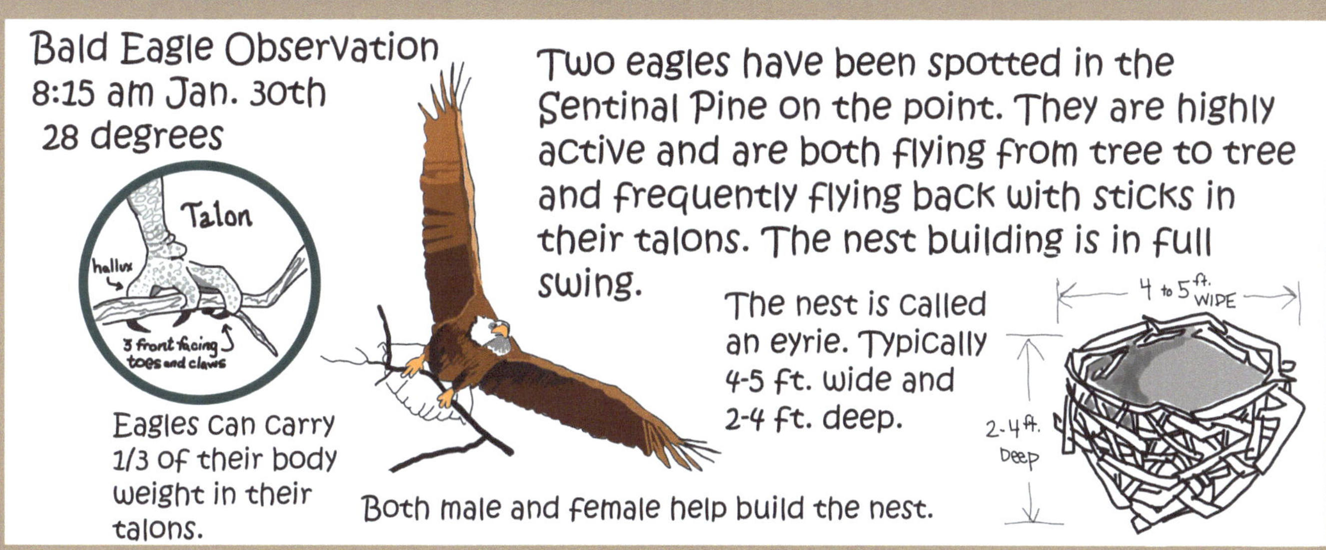

Keeping an Observation Journal is fun and easy to do. All you need is a notebook of any kind.

When you observe something in nature, grab your journal and a pen or pencil. In Annie's journal notice that she recorded the time, date, and the temperature. You can record what you think is important to know and remember.

After Annie observed the eagles, she researched some facts about what she saw. This added to her understanding and helped her grow to understand what she was seeing.

It is also so fun to look back and remember what you have observed and learned!

Observing Animals Around Us

```
H O P S S P E C T A C L E E Z
Y J O C V F O O T P R I N T S
M Q S H S C H A L L E N G E R
S X Q A J A F A J G R M M O C
L W U S H C N W A X A S A B G
M V A E N S A D J H N N Y S O
F E D L B H H M W N C O A E F
N L M M L Q Y E P I H W P R I
A J O O Z O R H R G C Y P V S
T W U A R U W E O I R H L E H
U A F N T I Z T S W F O E H I
R T T G G I E D A C L F U F N
E C T Z A L N S P I U I I N G
Q H B I F C E G F O L E N O D
B Z A L E A P I N G A Y P G Z
```

SWALLOWTAIL	CAMPGROUND	FOOTPRINTS
MEMORIES	MAYAPPLE	CHALLENGE
SPECTACLE	LEAPING	SANDWICH
HOWLING	SHERIFF	FLOATING
RESCUE	JUNGLE	NATURE
FISHING	OBSERVE	CHASE
RANCH	SNOWY	SQUAD
WATCH		

**Answers can be found on the
last page of this book**

Observation Match-up Game

Pet the Goose — **I**

Fireflies — **E**

Dog and Bunny "Leapfrog!" — **L**

My Bucket List: Dude Ranch Adventures — **B**

Kool — **K**

Don't Feed the Bears! — **G**

The Great Rescue — **A**

Deer Olympics — **C**

Sheriff Kathy and Flossie the Wonder Horse — **J**

The Elusive Otters of Lake Emory — **D**

Miss Sapphire — **H**

Footprints in the Snow — **F**

Word Search

Observing Animals Around U

```
H O P S S P E C T A C L E E Z
Y J O C V F O O T P R I N T S
M Q S H S C H A L L E N G E R
S X Q A J A F A J G R M M O C
L W U S H C N W A X A S A B G
M V A E N S A D J H N N Y S O
F E D L B H H M W N C O A E F
N L M M L Q Y E P I H W P R I
A J O O Z O R H R G C Y P V S
T W U A R U W E O I R H L E H
U A F N T I Z T S W F O E H I
R T T G G I E D A C L F U F N
E C T Z A L N S P I U I I N G
Q H B I F C E G F O L E N O D
B Z A L E A P I N G A Y P G Z
```